Dedication:

To John, McKenzie, Nicholas, Tyler, Jordan, Anna, Ella, Alexandra and Angelica
My Best Buddies, and true inspiration for Hugs and Kisses

XO XO XO

Fill every child's life with Hugs and Kisses

ISBN: 0615816002
ISBN-13: 9780615816005

Hugs and Kisses
Dont Fight Like Cats & Dogs

Book 1:
Be a Buddy Not a Bully

XO XO XO XO
Fill Every Child's Life with Hugs and Kisses!

The new adventures of Hugs and Kisses. Hugs: an enormous, easy-going, lovable brown & white St. Bernard - a colossal canine! Kisses: a petite, cuddly, affectionate, pure white Siamese - a stylishly graceful feline. They're best friends who refuse to fight like cats and dogs!

Story & Songs By:
Owen McGovern

Illustrated by:
Allie Surdovel

Hugs, a gigantic brown and white St. Bernard, and his best friend Buddy Beagle are prancing through Peaceful Park. Suddenly, they see Bully Bulldog chasing a cute, little, Siamese cat. "Hey Bully! Leave that little kitty alone," Hugs shouts. "Pick on someone your own size!"

"Aw, I'm just having fun, Hugs," Bully yells back. "Besides, she's not like us. She's just a creepy cat." "It's not nice to frighten others just 'cause they look different, Bully," Hugs scolds. "We should all be nice to one another."

"Dogs always chase cats and growl, Hugs," Buddy Beagle chimes in, "Don't you know that?" "That doesn't make it right, Buddy," Hugs explains. How would you like someone scaring you?"

"Who could scare me? Everyone's afraid of me," Bully boasts in a rough, tough voice.
"I'm not afraid of you, Bully," Hugs warns.
"Oh, Hugs, you're such a gentle giant. You wouldn't hurt a fly," Bully yells with a
great big belly laugh.

Hugs looks up at the defenseless little feline clinging to a shaky branch. "Don't be afraid little kitty, Bully won't hurt you," He says, in a warm, reassuring voice. "Who says I won't?" Bully challenges, growling at the terrified cat once more.

Hugs, who is twice as big as Bully, leans down and with one giant paw, picks him up by the scruff of the neck. "I say so, and I'm not afraid of you," He growls.

"I thought you were my friend, Hugs," Bully pleads with the colossal canine in a quivering voice.

"I am your friend, Bully," Hugs calmly assures him. "I'm just trying to show you how to get along with others so you'll have lots more friends."

"Please put me down Hugs. Don't hurt me," Bully begs in a frightened, shaky voice.
Now he knows how the frightened, little cat feels.
"I won't hurt you Bully," Hugs reassures him. "We should never hurt others. We should all be friends."

"Sure, Hugs, anything you say," Bully responds in a quivering, quaking voice as Hugs lowers him to the ground. He then notices Hugs smiling at him and lets out a sign of relief. Hugs really is his friend.

"Now, say you're sorry to my new-found, feline friend," Hugs commands.
"Sorry kitty," Bully responds, with a weak smile, looking up at the white, Siamese cat.
Hugs smiles, pleased by Bully's apology. "Now, wasn't that a nice thing to do?"

"Aw, this isn't any fun, anymore, anyhow. I'm going to the ballpark to chase baseballs, and growl at little kids," Bully boasts with a nervous laugh.

Buddy Beagle watches Bully prance off down the hill, and is totally confused. "Hey, Hugs. Why did you help that little kitty? She's just a cat, not like one of us? And she's a girl too!"

"It's much more fun when we all play together nicely," Hugs explains. "Lot's more friends, means lots more fun!"

"I just think dogs should stick together," Buddy explains. "Dogs should only play with dogs."

"You'll miss out on lots of new and different friends that way, Buddy," Hugs warns. "Maybe so, but I feel safer with my own kind," Buddy responds. "I think I'll go chase baseballs with Bully. Wanna come, Hugs?"

"No, I'll stay here and play with my new friend," Hugs says, as Buddy Beagle trots off to join Bully.

Hugs knows Buddy will like his new friend. Buddy likes everybody! And, everybody likes Buddy!

Bully still hasn't learned to play nice with others, though. But, since he was frightened too, maybe he won't be so mean.
"Be a Buddy, not a Bully," Hugs chuckles to himself.

Hugs waves to the frightened feline, shaking and clinging to a branch high atop the tree. "Come on down, little kitty. No one's gonna hurt you now," he shouts. "Bully's gone."

The petite, pure white, Siamese cat with blue eyes, and rhinestone collar cautiously climbs down. She's not afraid of this giant St. Bernard. He makes her feel safe. After all, he did rescue her from Bully.

"Hi. I'm Hugs. Everyone calls me that 'cause I give great, big hugs to all my pals."
"They call me Kisses 'cause I'm overly affectionate. I greet my friends with lickity kisses on the cheek."

"I hope we can be friends and play together nicely," Hugs responds.
"Our friends won't like that," Kisses warns. "Cats and dogs never play together."

"When they see us having fun together, they'll want to play too!" Hugs says with a grin. "Then, we can all be great friends!" Kisses responds with a warm smile.

That day, cats and dogs watched with surprise in their eyes, as a smiling Hugs & Kisses walked together side by side through Peaceful Park, and promised to teach all their friends to be Buddies, not Bullies!

Meet Hugs & Kisses and their circle of friends!

DOGS

Hugs: A huge, brown and white, St. Bernard – one of the most loveable, huggable creatures you could ever hope to meet. Sometimes, his "Hugs" are so overpowering, however, they knock you down or squeeze you til your eyes pop! Purely by accident, of course. Hugs would never intentionally hurt anyone. He may be big, but his heart is twice as big as he is. He's a gentle giant. Like all St. Bernard dogs, he likes to help others.

Buddy Beagle: He's a brown, white and black beagle who loves to run and play in the park. Everyone loves Buddy and Buddy loves everyone. He gets along with his people family, especially the children, and with other dogs. He is good-natured, and a loyal, and trusted friend who would never harm anyone. He's everyone's best Buddy. His best friend is Hugs. He follows Hugs everywhere and takes his advice.

Bully Bulldog: He's a light tan and white bulldog, with a mouth that scowls naturally, making him appear tough, and menacing. So, that's the part he plays in life. He believes it's his nature to be mean, tough and angry, and so he does everything in his power to live up to the reputation he's earned. He feels he would lose his identity if he acted any other way. Only Hugs can bring out Bully's softer side.

Penelope Poodle: This highly intelligent, well-groomed, well-mannered, large, white female poodle, sometimes gets carried away with herself, looking down on other dogs. She loves to wear a variety of colored scarves around her neck. Lime, purple, and orange are her favorite colors. She sometimes criticizes others, and makes them feel bad. But, she is quick to apologize and vow never to do it again – until the next time, of course.

Shamus (Red) Irish Setter: This good-natured, fun-loving Irish Setter is proud of his breed, and believes when it comes to canine royalty, the Irish are the noblest of the noble. He gets along with everyone, as long as they recognize his superior intelligence and dashing good looks. His friends call him Red which totally encourages him to show off the magnificent fiery red luster of his well-groomed coat.

CATS

Kisses: A warm, cuddly feline. An all-white Siamese cat with blue, piercing eyes, and a blue rhinestone collar. She has all the grace of a true princess as she promenades about, greeting friends with a soft meow and a bob of her head. Kisses is extremely affectionate and offers friends one of her lickety kisses. She loves all her animal friends, not just cats, but also birds, squirrels, and bunny rabbits. Even dogs! She's been that way since birth, so her family named her Kisses.

Calico Kate: A long-haired, female Calico cat with black, orange, and white patches. She has a streak of independence, makes outrageous statements, and is very opinionated, yet is also sensitive and caring. Kisses has a positive influence over Calico Kate, often pointing out her insensitive statements, which Calico is quick to apologize for. She is also aware of her beauty. And, like Kisses, doesn't brag about it.

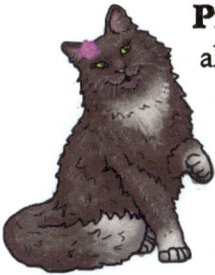

Pretty Kitty (Coco Cat): A York Chocolate semi-longhaired cat, with large, almond-shaped, green eyes, and a big fluffy tail and tufted feet, is considered a real beauty in the cat world. Her striking features stand out as she struts down the street, and people and animal friends alike always say, "what a pretty kitty." Hence, she is called Pretty Kitty by everyone. But she is self-centered, and always wants things. She is a "Me, Me, Me Meow cat! She is one of Kisses' best friends, along with Calico Kate.

Tomcat: He's a tough, feral cat who loves the freedom and independence of outdoors. His size frightens other cats, and his swagger and prowling mannerisms make other cats stay away. He doesn't always fit in because he has no family. But, Kisses is not afraid of TomCat. In fact, she reprimands him for his poor behavior at times. TomCat allows Kisses to boss him around, because secretly he would love to be part of a family. He has made Kisses and her friends his unofficial family.

www.ingramcontent.com/pod-product-compliance
Lightning Source LLC
Chambersburg PA
CBHW041240040426
42445CB00004B/98